Loose Magic

Les Bernstein

Finishing Line Press
Georgetown, Kentucky

Loose Magic

Publisher: Leah Huete de Maines
Editor: Christen Kincaid
Cover Art: Les Bernstein
Author Photo: Irving Bernstein
Cover Design: Elizabeth Maines McCleavy

Order online: www.finishinglinepress.com
        also available on amazon.com

Author inquiries and mail orders:
Finishing Line Press
P. O. Box 1626
Georgetown, Kentucky 40324
U. S. A.

Contents

VI
Naked Little Creatures

VII
Amid The Din

For my darling darlings

An Introduction

"Loose Magic." You are about to engage with Les Bernstein in a wide-ranging, deep exploration of what poetry can be in the hands and mind of a poet who has had no models, no teachers, no examples of what poetry should be. Here is poetry written by that rara avis (a rare bird) who appears suddenly and brilliantly with poems that touch you at your core and you can't explain how, that reach beyond expectation to say exactly what you were thinking but never had the words to express.

It is no wonder that her credits extend to dozens of journals, contests, Pushcart nominations. The truth is that despite never having read such poems before, selective editors and readers recognize genius when they come to it. I don't use that word loosely; Gertrude Stein admitted to having met only three in her lifetime, and she credited herself among them. Les is, in the world in which she lives, a poetic genius although she would be the last to acknowledge that fact.

In addition to writing dozens of poems that embody her poetic mastery, Les is also exemplary in recognizing how other poets might improve their poems, not by attempting to have their poems sound like hers, but to enable poets to improve their work, using her seemingly innate knowledge of how to do that, whether by re-ordering stanzas or by deleting superfluous words. Les has co-edited four collections of poems written by members of the large community of Redwood Writers of Sonoma County. She has also edited a beautiful collection of poems written by students in Marin County, California.

Among the pages in this collection of Les's work written over a lifetime, you will find exquisite poems that reach all of us who have laughed, who have loved and who have lost. "Loose Magic" contains the whole of life experience, never backing away from intensity, but elevating each instance to memorable heights.

Fran Claggett-Holland
Poet, Editor, Teacher

I

"Go beyond reason to love: it is safe.
It is the only safety."

Thaddeus Golas
The Lazy Man's Guide to Enlightenment

Step Right Up

happening in the center ring
a tight rope of ordinary human emotions
is hung with change and fate
the first step on will always be the hardest

choreographed by the unknowable
moments scaffold a too brief life
with its rhythms and tumults of dreams
the only certainty... gravity's triumph

although it starts so innocently
time does not hold us
the safety net is wonder
it is worth the price of admission

Advice from Mother on Your One Less Day

skip obligation's inescapable sins
wiggle out of pigeonholes
enjoy happenstance and flux
don't forget to floss

clog the clunky machinery of belief
refuse templates of self
ignore persistent memory
elbows off the table

airbrush your self portrait
invite farcical pratfalls
avoid hard labor's invitation to bruise
shoulders back stand up straight

one day a chill seeps into bones
clouds will scud at dusk
adventures of a single consciousness
turn to particle and ash

until then
navigate by lightless stars
hand write thank you notes
rsvp yes to everything

assumption

like an oncoming migraine
of radical acceptance
an instructive narrative notifies
the past uncloaked and humbled
is always a present now

a confiding whisper insists
to a swath of warm soft self
that permanence is covered
by a shroud of impermanence

born knowing only
a psalm of guessing
warring paradoxes
mutable and perplexing
seem as doomed as a cut flower

one minute sipping a kir royale
next moment starring in a cautionary
public service announcement
for endless unpredictable change
and unreliable explanations

real or imaginary
is there eternal oneness
a big soul with no beginning or end
when infused with defensive optimism
it's tempting to believe

I was told

I was told
gibbons experience irony
rats laugh when tickled
reality and its representations are in more than just miles

I think
speech swells around memory
time is always the lead character
indifferent cosmos demand the solitude of existence

I believe
a talmudic study of the office safety manual will insure immortality
dressing for the job you want will camouflage a tattered core
and the aspirations of small and grand larcenies are at full capacity

I know
the last five of the ten commandments are negotiable
the cradle of the natural world is in danger of tipping over
levitation during meditation is caused by the exhaustion of gravity

I suppose
good news is possible in this one for certain life
perception will always shimmy between wonder and reason
unassailable magic is afoot in a recognizable world

I really wish
for a pilot light in the soul's opaque depth
that Harry Houdini will return with a steady stream of telling details
and the choppy waters of age are more than a countdown to nothingness

Bifocals

the psychic said
he had made contact with my mother
she was wearing glasses
large ones
I was sure
she could lose those
in the afterlife
what about her hearing aids
where was she getting batteries
and her diabetic testing supplies
what about dialysis
were there kidney support centers
did she have to watch her salt intake
what about her compression socks
and her thyroid medication
and the tiny little anti depressant pill
she took
so she wouldn't mind dying
organ by organ
so much

Loose Magic

night falls dark
a day unspools
an undertow of exhaustion
closes the eyes

for just this now
the curve of time will not exist
nor the buzz of endeavor
with its industry and sweep

with tinkling bells
cargo straining at the seams
the caravan of loose magic
dreams into town

indifferent to perception
landscapes mine the subconscious
give wonder and irony the heave
divulge reverie in its many registers

here the dead live again
permeate and linger
reveal the shape of wind
here the dreamer is dreamed

too soon a clock alarms
a surfeit of life will stir and forget
while the caravan of loose magic
slips off to its next destination

I Really Should Have Asked

in the first dream
I really should have asked you
how to navigate a too bright world
as the glare of everyday life blurs the shadows

in the second dream
I should have asked
how to always be at the beginning
how to be more cloth than thread

I cannot remember
if you ever said
age is cruel
and littered with loss

and why didn't I ask
if and when perception stops
does the airtight cell of personhood
become a disposable story

but mostly I want to know
if you miss me

Recipes

toward the end
my mother taught
my father to cook
to saute onions
mix meat with egg
add her special sauce
ketchup
form a loaf
bake at 375
for 55 minutes

she worried
he would miss
her meatloaf
her roast chicken
her mashed potatoes
her over boiled carrots

quiet as a sigh
age has ambushed us all
our history is disposable
the more misremembered
the truer it becomes
this story cannot escape
its familiarity
a then   a now
a chasm unbridgeable

this much is true
it is me who tells her
he wont be
coming home

Dad's 99th Birthday

it is your birthday
I leave the windows open
watch the sunflowers turn to the sun
light a candle to guide your way

I remember the year
that time slithered away
the day unlike others
tangling into a hard knot

it is sun drenched summer again
with its sharp cornered sky
terrestrial business folds in on itself
I light this candle
to guide my way

I Have Been Thinking

I've been thinking about death lately
how the days fall over
and time seems more wide than long

I've been thinking about the grasp of darkness
how we don't always grow toward the light
and how the soul does not show in x rays

I've been thinking about the past
the coherence of reality
moments lit by their own moons

how the heart of things human shimmers
warps and unravels
yet stays a glorious thing

I've been listening
to the ineffable's systolic beat
marking time like a clock

I've been thinking about death lately
the extraordinary ordinary
the unknown unknowns

I have been thinking
it is not only birthdays
that pass each year

The Local Obituaries

for Davey/Davo/David

released from the dense knot of stable identity
relieved of unfinished earthly busyness
and provided a longview of shifting perspectives
the newly minted souls
unanchored from their moorings
slipped to a cushioned distance
and according to the daily news
passed peacefully to parts unknown

amid the tidy obituaries
human interest stories
national and local news
weather and movie timetables
on what page
in this squeeze of life
does one find the instructions
on how to rebuild
our hearts

the newspaper neglects to say
between shadow and substance
the shuttered home of you
will be a long season
the pall will pull hard
time will arch backwards
and streams of memory
engraved in our cells
will river throughout
a span too wide

She

for Tootsie

in the urgent present
a mind slips and slides
age has chipped away
at a hard forged colony of self

as insubstantial as smoke
she can no longer find familiar
her disjointed remembrances
do not hold
there is no family root
left in this barren ground

how she got here
or her children's names
has seeped through her
she has nothing but time
to sit on a bench
and feed pigeons
empty purse tucked
close to her side

in this wilderness
does she notice
the shadows pulling hard
on this far side
of vast

Bittersweet

a melancholy
        tumble
a private sanctum
of rarefied
treasure

this
secret cache
cherished
ephemeral
a backdrop now

bitter
sweet

Dark of Night

between shadow and substance
we unload a dusty backstory
some days generous with drama
we care to speak the same language
relieved of certainty
we are so here
that we do not know
where we are
our story is a simple one
with sting and tenderness
how small existence can feel
its joys and struggles
a blink of life in the dark

See the Moon that is not there

gaudy orgies of astronomical hope
light the sky
iron carbon oxygen nothingness

bugs dance by bio luminescence
super novas explode
laws of nature apply intermittently

knowledge of impermanence
beyond infinity
furrows the brow

The Much More

for Fran and Madge

when the world was new
they planted a flag in the much more
spread themselves into the future
below a limitless sky

they built their home
with care and optimism
ruddy with trust in sunny days
and shiny well being

they grew to other bigger homes
but they were vandalized by time
the truth of shortening days
spread its substantive shadow

as walls of memories crumbled
they had to learn to live lightly
their home now becoming
dust powder bone

there is nothing unique in this story
or life's commanding gravitational pull
they held hands tightly
for as long
as they could

Revision

a spark from the ash heap
bright and hot ignites
the poem
again and again

hidden in the darkest deep
written in sand
the poem
pearls around a piece of grit

tinkered at the core
circumspect and stunted
the poem
deletes to page white

Cue the Bagpipes

for Stuart

beyond the reach of words
a reliable tune is piped
sighs something tender
to begin a goodbye

time and impermanence
have derailed a universe
thready imperfect memories
unravel the weave of you

on this short short day
a eulogy captures and culls
edits reduce a lifetime
narrows and exhausts

let the pipes wail
in silence we hard listen
for the unrepeatable
you

Dancing with the Stars

earth laps the sun for now
time speeds without brakes
choreographed by the unknowable
faith with its limitations
dances with hope

II

"What am I doing on a level of consciousness where this is real"

Thaddeus Golas
The Lazy Man's Guide to Enlightenment

Today in Yoga

today in yoga
I reupholstered my furniture
planned a dinner party
rewrote a poem

is that my name?
he definitely said my name
it's something about breathing
BREATHING?
ooooh! He wants to know if I am breathing
OF COURSE I'M BREATHING!
I am definitely breathing

maybe I will make trout almondine
where did I put those color swatches?
I'm hungry
DEFINITELY trout almondine
do I have lemons?
capers?
do you need capers?

did he just say downward dog or upward dog
I wonder if like a dog
he can put his foot behind his head
and scratch his ears
do they do that because they have fleas?
or just because they can
isn't there a joke about licking balls?

is that my name?
again

Mourning Meditation

its been promised
in silence
there is sweep and substance
that all is connected
discernible and clear
Oprah and Deepak say
meditation will cure
all that ails me
Dan Harris says
I will definitely be
10% happier

so ... I shape a pause
in the distinct present
with a quickening resolve
put the phone on silent
banish the cat
place my buttocks on a cushion
close my eyes
set timer for 30 minutes
and
inhale
exhale

and then...
feral moments vacillate
between boredom and drift
memory tears
on thorns of regret
ghosts of want
embed in tiny desires
chatter words
rise and float
inflict riddles
that shallow the depths
miss only a laugh track
and now

something dark
is swishing its tail

its has been promised
in silence
that all will be connected
discernable and clear
but for me
TM is only missing the J

Mitzie Mitts Mitts Her Serene Catness
Our Inscrutable Fur Dominatrix

you are an enigma
a conundrum wrapped
in a paradox

why do you dart off like that???
what are you looking at???
we serve at your pleasure
do you not like the litter???
was it the food?

I know I stepped on your tail

sorry sorry sorry so sorry

we are all afraid of you
please don't pee on our bed

again

Judy G.

I saw Judy today
helmet askew
riding a tricked out bike
smiling
I saw her flash by
on that yellow 2 wheeler
even though
she never learned to ride
when she was alive

now I can hardly wait
to see my mother
waving from the lake
in a bright red bathing suit
holding with one sure hand
the pull rope
for her water ski
as she skims
the hilly wakes
like never before

No Cookies Involved

today I lost Gertrude Stein
she was gone for nearly 8 hours and 39 minutes
I remembered her thick ankles
the autobiography she wrote for Alice B.
and of course I did remember
Alice and her cookies
also I recalled how mean
thick ankled Gertrude was
to Hemingway's wife
hell… to all the wives
when she returned
in the Whole Foods parking lot
I could not keep
from screaming her name
and in general
being peeved with her
and her whole deal
a rose is a …
seriously?

Eat This Before Bedtime to Prevent Alzheimers

uh...
back in this room again   why?
ok... go back to where I was before
why am I here again?
am I missing anything?
keys, glasses, phone, sanity?
why am I writing this?
has the world tipped?

it's just that...
remembrance softened
to a satin pillow that smothers
it's a disparate theory of nothing
even the ghosts are confused

should I walk backwards?
eat with my non dominant hand?
do puzzles?
shoot birds on Lumosity?
sleep more?
socialize?
Gingko Biloba?

they say...
to prevent Alzheimers
there are things to do
they say
it's not the fall
that hurts

Billboard for Rent

for Lawrence Ferlinghetti

with a well lit hustle
and one sticky slogan
on a high trafficked area
let **us** help
mesmerize

lacking only
musical accompaniment
let **us** herald
what to buy
where to go
what to do

let **us**
address time's ravages
and compromised dreams
with the consolation
of a new purchase

let **us**
with euphoric
impossible to ignore
arch and winking aspiration
fill the yawning void

Call today
1 888 GET MORE

Heroes

they laughed
at the hapless and naive customers
all those easy marks
with their childlike trust
and hope in luck and fortune

they laughed
at their source of new income
at their ingenious son
so clever and cunning
so nobody's fool

they laughed
at the huge jar of jellybeans
he set on the counter next to the register
right below the no shoes no shirt no service sign
and they laughed at the new poster
GUESS THE NUMBER OF JELLYBEANS
win $100.00
a $1.00 a guess

they laughed
proud of their boy
as they made their deli meat sandwiches
smoothed mayo and mustard
placed lettuce, tomato, onion, and pickle
even added a napkin
they said "hey, it's life...
it ain't no contest
there ain't no winners"
$318.00
"that's nothing to laugh at"

The Slowly Cooked Stew of the Unknown and the Unknowable

1 lb mortal matters
1 cup edge of awareness
1 cup outskirts of identity
1 can unreliable compass
1 tablespoon infinite complexities of mind
2 heaping teaspoons insistence on the trivial
diced bulb of unfulfilled expectations
small slice of jarring interruption
grated rind of unanswered needs
pulverized string of indignities
bunch of revealing contradictions
pinch of central mystery

ceaselessly sift ingredients
add liquid conclusions
put lid on subtle worlds
simmer through generations

season to taste

This Year

corks pop with
fizzy sentiments
and celebration

time unadorned
backlit with occasion
algorithms and blues
played in a minor key

words overburdened
tinker with resolutions

strictures loosen
fuzzy and optimistic
a still recognized self
wishes all
a different new year

Come Sit Stay

for Mouse

> "Dogs are well known for their ability
> to backtrack to a beloved home—or person"
> C.   Clairborne Ray

a departure seen coming
yet sudden as a sneeze
strays to an inevitable story
pulls on the leash
of vertiginous sorrow

you have traveled too far
and I've become untethered
can you
will you
find me
will there be a time
we border and greet
again

will you come
if I whisper your name
in a language
with only
one speaker
left

Stay

for Matt's Magoo

on this colorless morning
a fog refuses to lift
between shadow and substance
dark is calling to dark

pulsing with resignation
time is circular
a resolute everyday
the same until it isn't

ambushed by age
your tail barely wags
they say it is the right thing
they say it is the kind thing

now in stinging brightness
how small existence seems
a slumberous slip from life
a quiet grows louder

nothing outlives the familiar
we flare and we fade
in all time   in every time
it ends on an exhale

we arrive here
so soon
and I cannot write
your name

Dutchess
Gypsy
Fivey
Sadie
Amos

Elwood
Jake
Mouse

Trick or Treat

ring the bell
and don't get caught
there are monsters
in the basement
quiet as a thought

bracketed by the dark
is life's drift and mystery
nothing but noise
a disposable history

as involuntary as a hiccup
the clock endlessly circles
claims further territory
brooks no reversal

amid sunshine and smiles
a need to masquerade
a multitude of heartbeats
permits this charade

so trick or treat
and here is the clue
tick tock
tock tick

boo

III

"I wouldn't deny this experience to the One Mind"

Thaddeus Golas
The Lazy Man's Guide to Enlightenment

Your Call is Important … Please Hold

as chaos remains
at a coiled remove
the delicate fiber of decency
frays and unravels

as mayhem grows
there are prayers
for compassion
from earnest hearts

entreaties are made
while petition laced
with honest hope
can only murmur and chirp

could the response
of no response
be the unbridgeable chasm
of an enduring shrug

is only empty static
the background muzak
of inaction
and indifference

who or what agent
will intercede
will humanity
answer the call

The Archangel of Damage

the world was once new
peopled with the industrious
hoping themselves into a future
planting their flag in the much more

under impassive stars
they constructed houses
built with dust
and vandalized by inertia

even in sunlight
below a limitless sky
the haze of shortening days
cast substantive shadows

they prayed to the absolute dark
snatched at happiness to fill the gaps
yet nothing changed
though so much happened

well ... you get the idea
in the muddle
of the familiar
they never saw him coming

Beelzebub's Fundamentals for Success

for the Donald

operate from ego and bias
espouse sureness in an unfamiliar world
fill days with pretense of control
scatter seeds of religious certainty
ruminate on sour recrimination
deny the restless sifting of inevitability
demand an overly decorated future
speak with clicking sounds of errant thoughts
chafe against all that is good
tweet tweet tweet

It's That Time Again

multi candidate choices
yammer to be the solution
yammer to be the change
history is littered with their aspirations

end stage reckonings are presented in a rosy hue
inconvenient facts remain sheathed in duplicity
this color coordinated spectacle
is guaranteed to excavate seams of hope

as they pantomime larger than life family values
heavy production camouflages
the gummy web of personal failings
myopic confidence hits all requisite marks

it's that time again
so...
in a cross your fingers and hope not to die
don't forget to vote

What !?

Who looks outside dreams, who looks inside awakes. Carl Jung

outside the knowable
in the great dimming
does a pre-assigned destiny
cater to a fixed star
where is the wise narrator
where is the resilient hero

an obstinate sun circles and dawns
the tug of unexplainable
bumps against hard limits
conviction shifts between
the real and the invented
mentation fussy and belabored
leads to medicated pain relief

a clown car of wish and hope
is on a very narrow bridge
the loosening of certainty
has a real sting in its tail
could a hands up shrug
be the meaning of life

Damp Matches

as earnest as a pew
hope shrugs off a straight jacket
makes peace with the dark
and keeps on hoping

against time's ravages
and consolations
with rose tinted confidence
hope avers

as dark jokes go
with everything but a laugh track
hope knows the by and by
will be different this time

with wholesome sincerity
informed by faith in miracles
hope plans to light the way
but the matches are damp

At Sea

oceans rise and fall
shores vanish and appear
a house with no foundation
floats on hope and ideas

set on and off course
above an undertow pull
sea-scarred battered and tossed
our own particular whirlpool

in a sea shaken home
wishes ebb and flow
dreams wax and wane
people come and go

adrift in place
below sun and moon
a ballast of self
wishes to anchor soon

IV

"This, too, can be experienced
with a completely expanded awareness"

Thaddeus Golas
The Lazy Man's Guide to Enlightenment

City of Angels

we flew to Los Angeles to see the top specialist
the building and facility impressive
shown immediately to an office
we met the doctor's doctor
he was so knowledgeable
and informative
but
there was nothing to be done
no new protocol
no trial
as we gathered our stuff
my pad for notes
our jackets
he said
wait
tell me how you two met

The Chemo Chronicles

and here is the thing
in the used to be
nothing was to be interrupted
nothing was to be derailed
but in these countdown years
of accruing losses
as things fall away
what mattered once
is irrelevant now

make no mistake
the chaos of errant cells
bake into back burner anxiety
quash the blurry ephemera of dreams
meaning is similarly depleted
with dubious data
and indifferent definitions of success

this is an unenviable story
and I am not sure
what more to include
what to withhold
about chemicals deployed
that scope for direction
in a seeming abyss
life is just cliché arbitrary
held in our fragile vessels
and so shallow
is our footprint

5/17/19—5/11/20

this is what I carry
a crystal
my dad's handkerchief
my parents' wedding rings
false positivity
false smiles
false calm demeanor
I can no longer deny
we're at time's precipice

diminishing expectations
new doctor
new test
new protocol
damage
damage
damage
hope
for what
even they
so little
believe in

scudding between
chance's slippery dare
and fact's hard embrace
I can only see in reverse

you ask what I know
I believe in so much less
a disembodied voice
says sorry
It's not what we hoped

in what if's shorthand
I tell no one
there is more time
a loud silence echos back

my worry appears
like a sleeve caught on a thorn
its mobius rumination
leads nowhere
leads everywhere
what secrets pulse below
outward appearances
feats and failures of wishes
raze and rebuild
on a hourly basis

the lows so low
the highs not high enough
I want for us all
to be safely buckled
on a gentler ride

I tell no one
our stay won't be long
this chafing province of only sunset
lures from distraction and hope

thru the wormhole
of magical thinking
I post for prayer
I post for intents
ask the many "friends"
I do not even know
I call on the angels
I call on the ancestors

they do not come
we are alone
so alone

in this prolonged winter
more often
I tell no one
I am the hero
I am the victim
I wish it were me

infection
wires monitors tests
doctors nurses
machines
beep
beep
beep
afraid afraid afraid
in this house
once safe
I say please   please
don't let go of my hand
please   please   please
stay
with me
with me

sometimes in the mid night
his pills emptied into my hand
I wish for total blackness
wonder about selfishness
I know not yet
I want to abide
as long as he does
I wonder

have I the strength
to remain and linger
for the deeply loved
others

chaos
plaster deities
cement saints
medical stasis
waiting
waiting
for what
hospice angels

small tasks
overwhelm
I put my car in a ditch
now it thumps hard
just like my heart
crammed and raw
I try to ignore
imagine less
tight coils of evidence
I try to go
I try not to go
where the silence is

between crises
the wary soft spot
of practical tactics
consumes time
with routine

I stream Netflix
for episodic amnesia

serialized respite
I can exhale
55 minutes at a time
for now

for close to 40 years
Jammie the squirrel
has lived in our tree
what is the secret
to his longevity
could it be
belief's magic

was it ten little Indians
then there were nine
but what about
the ten little monkeys
jumping on the bed
and the one that fell off
and broke my heart

what becomes of the beheld
without the beholder
it's an everyday magic act
with limited variations

my navigator is gone
the direction only away
lost in the vast unnameable
I float in liminal space

in the churn of this spinning world
there is evidence everywhere
loving hard is unsafe and doomed

a difficult dog to keep on the porch

walled in between 2 ears
I spin so slowly
and stay in place
my dilemmas
so very ordinary

memory's lure and distraction
a backward pull of drift
threads but also needles
dark corners and sparks of light

bright and ringing hunger for familiar
gnaws in the unsettled territory of days
marshaling from a dark reservoir
the sneaky tenderness of time

feathers butterflies pennies rainbows
that sound is it a name whispered
mutable signs or magical thinking
what cast if any do specters take

maybe I travel too far
reaching the margins of true
I become this place
inhabit this new land

415 306 2402
what message could I leave
you were my home
there is no elsewhere

another kind of silence
reveals more than it hides
this insistent quiet
heavy in the bones

living in the present tense
a hidden secondary self
robed in hopeful colors
struggles to exhale

in the four corners of the unnameable
an insistent and steady pulse
listens devoutly to the silence
wants a future worth wanting

The World We Share

living in different light
the pull of shadows
mess and noise
cleaves in half
a before
an after

my home was you
the world we shared
willfully ordinary
kept the time
out of time

always a risk
bright and hot
the bulwark instinct
to hold and keep
sparking
remembering
love invisible

To Answer Rachel's Question

I do not know much
about this world
what is a neutrino
what is an axion
is dark matter anything other
than what is between my ears

I do know this
grief is not mannered and quaint
it' s deep and unfeigned
a riot in the soul
it walks unstable terrain
finds no foothold

perplexed by spirits
words I write
chisel their way
rise and shimmy
hope for consolation
long for distraction
but simply
they just pile up

scudding clouds current
a sharp cornered sky
while an obstinate sun
always circles and dawns
the tides go out
may they not return

neutrino
a neutral subatomic particle with a mass close to zero and half-integral spin, rarely reacting with normal matter.
axion
a hypothetical elementary particle postulated by Peccai-Quinn theory in 1977

How to Build a Heart in the Rushed Momentum of Later Life

it is useful to know
the ashes of legacy
raddled with knotty uncertainty
will exert a sturdy hold

reconsidered in light and in shadow
the curious operations of fate
insistent and unruly
should be swept into the dustpan

grappling with the ineffable
in the too short lapse of being
a voice calling itself I
lives at its own risk

a wordless backstory progresses
no moment ever the same
it is just life
and then it is over

for now
it is best to remember
I was here
and I loved

More Holes than Fabric

a magic too subtle
for messy entrances
my dead must wait
and abandon visible time

they tell in tongues
attempt irrefutable signs
wish enough ballast
to emerge in the knowable

they have cued
grief is love after loss
and the earth will
shake us off like fleas

they hover and flit
enter my dreams
while I am still tethered
to this material world

Our Abbreviated Time

in the thrum of treadmill days
we clasp our joys
and endure our sorrows
while squalls of forgetting
blur the mystery of it all

for big hand little hand lives
a clock ticks inaudibly
marking the indifference of time
in a realm of consistent transience

sunlight dims to night
a humble old moon
has seen it all
will see it again
and again

in the erratic and unpredictable theatre of hope and wishful thinking Irving Bernstein appears simultaneously in multiple locations

Connie declares you are in the corner of her office guiding her hands with her patients
while Jacqueline says you are on the couch rooting with her for the home team
Elizabeth promises you showed up as a red fox and have been instrumental in helping with her finances
Phil reports you continue to hike the Marin trails with him every Saturday
Howie swears you want another rematch of Rumi Cube
Judy insists she waves at you standing in her bedroom doorway but you never wave back
Gregory writes you talk often and are giving him a tutorial on love
Joy testifies you twinkle in the sky when she looks up at night
yet I say the heft on your side of the bed is the pillows that I pile there
and that you have not mentioned
that sometimes I wear the same clothes day after day
or my paralysis of will to break this fall
and that your coffee cup spins my world off axis
but what do I know of the afterwards
or the reverent quiver of belief
only once you appeared in my dreams
and it was to simply express
that you did not want
Chinese chicken salad

Saturday Evening

for Irving

I see them
at the restaurant
an aluminum walker
with green tennis balls
on the bottom
an easier push
it leans against a near wall

they are so very old
I wonder would I just stay home
but here they are
still together
their heads unintentionally bowed
almost touching
they are in companionable silence
it is with ordinary awe
I envy them

Angel M.I.A.

"Every blade of grass has its angel that hovers over it and whispers grow, grow" —A Rabbinic commentary

in a dark corridor
the last speaker of a familial language has died
leaving only tangles and absence

attendant ideas and torrents of anecdotes
cannot translate seamlessly
what lies beneath gleaming surfaces

you once said believe those who seek truth
doubt those who are certain of it
cover them like a parrot you wish to silence

you said looking outside is a dream
a convenient fiction
good luck with that

tell me who is going to
teach radiant oneness
be a beacon incandescent and alive
who will whisper
grow

Heliotropism

I am dreaming
always dreaming
a protagonist sleepwalking
these most ordinary chapters
of thought's well-worn grooves

things will always happen
an anarchy of experience
mess and distraction
bountiful and inexhaustible
in my epic novel
no one is reading

to tell a little bit of truth
here is a non-fiction version
my story is my story
my story is just a story
my story is not true

will the sleepwalker awake
to an illuminated darkness
no foothold in the mutable past
no mindless march into ephemera

can there finally be
the silencing of language
the inner symphony
with only one sustained note
of full throated living

just simple
so simple
being
and not
so simple
being
in the soft glow
of an eternal now

V
The Chapbooks

Borderland

"Love as much as you can from wherever you are."

Thaddeus Golas
The Lazy Man's Guide to Enlightenment

Somersault

something rare
has happened

robed in
strenuous denial
metaphors
take to the air
somersault
backwards

swift
unexpected
plain speak
announces
fallen souls
headed
for a landing

Hard Denial

the laws of delusion
mandates trouble
twists
reversals
willed forgetting

the laws of fabrication
unsettles circumstance
denies cause
exists on the margins

the laws of concoction
author's fiction
belying
a present tense

the laws of possibility
blank and unscripted
invent and pursues
a different path

Galaxies

galaxies form
blurry specks
burn brightly

hydrogen
helium
mysteriously cool

elements gather dust
small and irregular
below
the threshold
of detection

stars form
and
light
a dim
distant
past

Borderlands

late
into the night
a slow moon
transits

reflects
upon
itself

borderlands
slip by
become
slowly older

tomorrow's
unknowable
day
makes
something
bloom

Should You Awake

should you awake
in a tumult of dream
narrow the lens of
slippery glimpses
move simply to
heart catching
rhythms
wend carefully
the bruises
of brambles
give blessings to
crumbled moorings
build a refuge
on clouds of dust
summon and capture
an epic story
remain intact
return to sleep

The Bride   The Groom

aware of the photographer
they stand together
a prologue
of nuanced hopefulness
a woven
dense history
deep rooted
in identity
personal stories
pictured in stills
fixed in place
an absence
of full understanding
an early harvest
of future
disappointments
they stand
side by side
unaware
of one another's
tender   tender
heart

Routine

the narcotic
of unfailing habits
numbed by routine
insistent logic
transparent
enmeshes
entangles

a life apart
like any other
it's own oasis
a crowded realm
of eccentricity
lived in the round
haunted by joy

Bulbs

gardener of small
domestic miracles
planting
enough for a lifetime
      before
ground freeze
       and
winter's stealth
       between
belief
and
delusion
bulbs hidden
in dirt
on a sunshined windowsill
flower   an early spring

Intoxicated

they toasted life
the sweet jam at the center
a celebration of
early victories
and preliminary results

inside their bubble
a storied past
a carefully scripted present
awaits
like a weather report

an incursion
from the rebellious
lowlands

Broken

typically
there is heartbreak

storms and divides

tiny fissures
open wide

discontent settles
wedges deep

lives realign
unsanctified

alone   together

Golden Gate

tourist
destination
cliffs
towering
drops
stripped away
lone figure
ponders
imperatives
hesitations
a storm of
human error
unmoored
adrift
plucked
from
the sea

Rocking Chair

life lived from a rocking chair
dispels the aura of relevancy
the pull of stability and change
sway to their own pace
chapters are forgotten
distilled and compressed
life accelerates
it is truth no longer shocking
inner voices dwindle
filling untended space
gone in a blur
personal history
vivid
various
and
vast

Final Match

there are tennis balls
not in tournaments
or neighborhood courts
but on the bottom
of aluminum legs
that scrape along
walkways and floors

game
set
match

no trophy
no shaking of hands
a high net gets higher

step
push
step

Time Unspools

days tumble by
days standstill
memory and prophecy
collapse

a hazy sameness
foretells
a borderless
self

torn from all
scavenging alone
the sum of life
passes through
unattended
space

Dottie

little brittle bird bones
wearing no one's clothes
sitting in no one's chair
feeding on air and light

a heart beats because
it does not know how
to stop

a mouth opens for a long ago
mother

the dream is almost over

blue veins map a topography of
distant neighborhoods
and a faraway nowhere

time repeats itself
time repeats itself
time repeats itself

as if it mattered.

Ruth

Ruth inhabits a
time of senses
names none

meaningless stories
summon
at random
unruly emotions

a child
a sister
a mother
no longer

her orphaned soul
in dark play
walks backward
thru shadows
goes nowhere
   slowly

Winter

as days shorten
an ordinary life
of unfathomable mystery
longs for communion

restless ghosts
circle and abound
hover nearby
then drift away

even a hardened heart
trailed by spirits
wishes to slow
the candle

The Daily News

reading the obituaries
the world goes on
at a far center
a universe dies
a compression of lifetimes
into words
sometimes
a photo
of someone
smiling

Tumbleweed

stories are told
the narrative
suspicious
the mind's echo chamber
vast and uncooperative
offers images
far from origin
tumbleweed moments
of a lost tribe

VI

Naked Little Creatures

Everyday

every day in the middle distance
I build my house
the foundation yoked to plausibility
a dreamscape yard

underneath a waking life
a charmed unconcern
makes sacred
altars for ordinary life
rooms built for forgetting

every day I build
a structure from the roof down
beams high
a hint of dry rot

every day I build
strange mysteries of small benedictions
a story carved in bone
no matter how unique
not exactly new

Bitter Feast

it was hard ordering the world
the hive of activity
the naming of all

the whiff of mystery
the garnish of holiness
some breezy embellishments
a bitter feast

selective forgetting
begets cautious optimism

haphazard conclusions
beget ordinary life

probably foretold
the snake will
devour its tail

The Balloon Escapes the Grasp

on a day like any other
a tale veers elsewhere
in a trusted cloud of confidence
the balloon escapes the grasp

a short tether
of mayfly life
slips and disappears
enters the bellies of stars

something raw and tender
searches upward
tallies the distance
of measured impermanence

against all evidence
alive in every color
globes of optimism
glow in the sky

Milk Bone

crumbs in my pocket
we walk so slowly

smells no longer interest you
your world is reduced to me

I am your religion
and I will betray you

we walk to this edge together
we will both fall far

Late Night Elegy

somewhere along the way
life passed into sameness
boundaries meandered and pooled

the link was broken
between spirit and matter
flesh and reveries

illuminated by insight
the geometry of us
wide awakened

our small world
phased out of orbit
and a larger universe
trumpeted forth

Naked Little Creatures

exiled into the world
self-replicating versions of the miraculous
hover and buzz

bracketed by stars so far apart
refracted parables of daily life
flutter and fuss

busy beeping lives
come and go

uncertainty is punctuated with a question mark
gravity will never change its mind

intoxicated by its own mystery
implausible happiness
attracts a crowd

This Time

details grim
decisions hard
no solace
of small comforts

what remains
tubes
needles
pumps
machines
a television
droning

hope
hard to lose
peace
hard to find
grief is ascendant

time moves fast
time moves slow
time stops
time moves
    on

The Today Show

a congenial group
of skilled practitioners
come to congress

governing with glory
false starts
hectoring
quarrels and vexations
they scythe their way

the judgement comes quickly
the solution   easy
other's suffering
will require forgetting

Nothing Nulls the Clock

again and again
calendars shed pages
seasons blur
life winds down

the stalwart pair
mother nature
father time
slough off
residency of selves

outskirts of identity
are traveled and crossed
biography becomes alphabet

notions of the invisible
flutter like strange mysteries
moments drift lightly

pondering the miraculous
emptied out days
unpinned
fly away

Dad

you
were of a generation
who dressed up for
doctor appointments
airline flights
dinner on Sunday night
and
your operation

you
were of a generation
who loved the flag
revered doctors
told corny jokes
to orderlies
nurses
people in white coats

you
a good patient
unfailingly polite
found belief easy
trusted the system

and now
what is left
your good black trousers
black v neck sweater
fresh white shirt
and brand new shoes
in a white plastic bag

Irrevocable Weather

funnel clouds gather
windows are shuttered
the airiest of sighs
rattles the door

question unasked
leave all to imagination
prayers and incantations
can not shed light upon dark

birds are not born with melody
they learn songs from others
grief has its own music
unteachable yet known

with the pull of shadows
life seeps through us
we cover the mirrors
a slow joining of hands

Time in Jeopardy

a hidden self
robed in uncertainty
inhales the past
skids into the future

nostalgic concerns
slated for demolition
forsake
broader truths

conclusions
caged in longing
flutter and buzz
like a trapped fly

Lacking a Proper Helmet

a life gets built
intent on erasing
dark sentiments
tangled feelings
a howling void
questions are inevitable
extinct tongues
babble
history bears down
more sum
less parts
scattered hopes
grow lighter

life's rush and crash
random   inexplicable
tugs past into present
no voice will guide
thru the decades
human talking points
serve as a warning
winking quotation marks
will narrate chronicles
elaborate a fiction
rendered true

All Old Men

all old men look like my father
stand at the pharmacy counter
in exactly the same way
their images already sepia and grainy

all old men walk the supermarket aisles
push step by step the basket
with two bananas and one can of soup
move slowly to the edge of the frame

all old men fish thru their pockets
for change at the post office
buy less than five stamps
for messages to a world left behind

a shadow faces a distant wall
my dear old man
appears in a familiar landscape
Dad, turn around

In the Lull

natural insurgencies
fill
stretched time

uncertain journeys
swear
never to reveal

the mystery

simple

happiness and despair
constant as nightfall
dwell side by side

Ordinary Light

for Irving

one small risk
at a time
bright and hot
everywhere
invisible

a bulwark instinct
to hold and keep
cleaves in half
a before
an after

living in different light
the pull of shadows
mess and noise
home
is you

this world we share
willfully ordinary
takes the time out of time

Sleep

a milky sky darkens
a furious little world
winds down

edges smooth
hum with relief

thickened dreams
drift magic
reach thru the night
lag into morning

vast and slippery
time's shifting weight
navigates the rings of Saturn

Forty Winks

it is late in a day
governed by predictable rules
and tight bunches of activity

a hollow thrum of deep space sound
says just enough
yet not enough to answer
what lies within and without

let the myths keep changing
outside knowledge and control
the whooshing sound of mystery
hums unremittingly below the surface

the miraculous oddness of existence
drifts into tidy nighttime routine
while pillars of dust
incubate newborn stars

an endless chain of moments
of immutable now gathers velocity
until one more time
becomes today

The Trickster Side of Language

ambient unease
a knotty matter
a sharpened pinch
unfolds between

conversations
mill and low
cannot reconcile
fiction and truth

emptied out days
flee the center
one final look back
see what you want

15 Minutes

the wages of fame
are paid with rough magic
the pull of the spot light
shifts and bends

unheard melodies
provide the soundtrack
humming an epic
chutes and ladder life

the curve of forgetting
unconcerned with survival
discards a biography
more invented than planned

fame's terrier yap
indifferent to reputation
deafen's the world
with abundant small thought

even posterity has a shelf life
the meter is running
obscurity will wait

Afoot in a Conventional Story

when all was well
time passed imperceptibly
clots of concern were placed aside

did we expect to be parted
be near the far
allowed only other dreams

decades drifted by
lives uprooted from the bottom
fitted together   slipped apart

a second slower look
in sunset light
closed the circle

in the rear view
a full turn
once around
when all
was well

The Hard Work of Whimsy

For the poets

undetected muses
wander light years
leave tender impressions
go dreamy in life

day after day
arranging convergences
threading together
a particular earth
a lasting moon

wide hearts
alive in every color
happy with shaping
galaxies of dust

pulse and shimmer
with earthly oddness
softly underline
a luminous unknown

When I Die

I will find
my cellphone
favorite sunglasses
my wrinkle free face
my sense of humor

when I die
a shoe box of dangerous cliches
fleshy and heartfelt
will conjure my earthly side

when I die
the din of expectations will quiet
and a thin rhapsody
will sigh a single bright flower

when I die
a fitful flame will evaporate
gauzy mists of light and heavy words
the precise geometry of details

when I die
my old dog will bark
then sing to the moon
of birth and death
and the everything
in between

VII

Amid the Din

Sewing Lesson

between clouds and abyss
the garment of self
is sewn with the patient enemy time

beyond the hem of language
a selected collision
of eloquence and gibberish
tailor the world we live in

fashioned of earth
embellished with moon
the tight suit of existence
is darned to follow its own light

In Our Story

enclosed within
the high grey wall of late years
miles of words shift underfoot
clouds creak and groan

maps fail a horizontal plain
landmarks vanish
geography bends

in this punch of a story
gods beg devotion
as they thin the herd

time is a ghosted guide
weightlessly wandering the future
taking us where we least expect

Come Summer Stay Summer

a hint of winter drifts into focus
the earth's rotation slows
according to the arc of the sun
life is drawn with a hazy outline

in the banalities of age
elliptical lessons of daily existence
progress a too short lapse of being

choreographed by the unknowable
paced with narrative suspense
a reluctant history
can only try to understand
the inky infinite that brackets life

While

in the thrum of treadmill days
squalls of reasonableness
blur the mystery of it all

clocks tick inaudibly
the here and now
the then and there

teachers might have mentioned
the riddles unsolvable
while the humbled old moons
can't help but grin

A Fitful Flame

in heaven underground
an ordinary shimmer
can turn sudden spark
flaring the vast unknown

here and elsewhere
faith is an experiment
home in the dark corners
hatching stars from dust

each day indifferently holy
loosens human contours
has its sacrifices
carries its secrets close

Now I Lay Me

searching for one enduring livable truth
a nighttime tourism of the country between
coaxes messages from deep center

an internal voice serving as a narrator
sighs soothing delusions of a coherent self
trying to lullaby fundamentals of existence

fuzzy with kinks and quirks
a dream unfolds
clicking into place an unsusceptibility of awe
for a world marbled with the familiar
awaiting in the morning

According to the Arc of the Sun

drawn with a hazy outline
and too tender for the task
a life tries to make sense of a natural world

years grounded in air
and lived in the round
conspire to hide
the battered marvel of the mundane

nights will grow longer
the earth's rotation will slow
a hint of winter will always drift into focus

this much is certain
sliding from day to night
time will winnow without sentimentality
bisecting a now from then

Intent on Restoring Disorder

history lumbers on
unstoppable
insinuating
while birds and everyone else
sing the same phrases
over and over

fleeing angels correct their course
seeking a fresh exit strategy
as the dung beetle orients itself
by the light of the milky way
its life as flat as a comic strip

the clouds whisper to each other
left only to bear witness
they sigh the name
of the space in between

although details are in dispute
time goes by
in an amnesic drift
the past with exultation and ache
anticipates the future's return

Someone Left the Gate Open

living without pause
the beast of inflated personal history
sniffs and roams
barks and howls

even in the larger yard
where all the bones are buried
he doesn't just dig
but defecates on sacred ground

with little use for words
he scavenges with hubris
only pleasing sounds register

the leash of life
may still be loose around his neck
but even the defiant will fetch and heel
and perhaps play dead

The Small Ordinary

days darken earlier at the slack end of life
there is time to troll the blur of the past
revisit the tiny desires of our own design

seeking practical tips for impending conclusions
messages from the unconscious
hear licks and riffs of the incomprehensible

the earthbound mend of recognizable gestures
fail to slow propulsive inevitability

the only salve is to love
anything
beyond
reason

Unvarnished

my mother said
when the morning sky is pink
the circus will come to town

my mother never explained
moon splattered stories
laid out frame by frame
edges smoothed and tucked away

my mother never believed
the hazy terrain of
theories
diagnoses
predictions

my mother trusted
life's murky plot
held in service
of an unvarnished reality

my mother expected
night to fall hard
the circus
to move on

Testimony

I was told
gibbons experience irony
rats laugh when tickled
reality and its representations are in more than just miles

I think
speech swells around memory
time is always the lead character
indifferent cosmos demands the solitude of existence

I believe
a talmudic study of the office safety manual will insure immortality
dressing for the job you want will camouflage a tattered core
and the employment of small and grand larcenies are at full capacity

I know
the last five of the ten commandments are negotiable
the cradle of the natural world is in danger of tipping over
levitation during meditation is caused by the exhaustion of gravity

I suppose
good news is possible in this one for certain life
perception will always shimmy between wonder and reason
unassailable magic is afoot in a recognizable world

I really wish
for a pilot light in the soul's opaque depth
that Harry Houdini will return with a steady stream of telling details
and the choppy waters of age are more than a countdown to nothingness

A Baptism in Time

in ether chill
hands hold a heart
its shivering home
the operating theatre

metal filigrees through
the broken places
upward and deep
it stirs and lulls

bits of memory
inherit the moment
in slow time
shut doors left ajar

nevermore's hard birth
begets days unlike others
beneath our breastbones
a sadness of ash

Dearly Beloved

we safe distance here for …
the sputtering exhaustion of daily briefings
the contamination of false condemnation and blame
an infested mind's prescription of Lysol and Clorox
with insane prophecies of healing and quick fix
yet as of today
with lukewarm hopes for a new normal
we safe distance
wear our masks
wash our hands
and mourn
the unfathomable deaths
with more to come

...And Yet

bonobos use symbols to communicate
border collies know 1,000 words
dolphins have a rudimentary number sense

crows make sophisticated tools
elephants recognize themselves in mirrors
reptiles have their insanely good looks

resembling a bloated kielbasa with dentures
the naked mole rat runs forward
and backward at the same pace

if their mate is unattractive
the zebra finch unwilling to propagate
lays smaller unsurvivable eggs

the bower bird enjoys decorating
with flowers and bright colors
no plaid is involved

and for human phenomenon
your unsayable absence
reduced to a bald plot
plumbs the futility of grief

Whenever

whenever in dreams I see my dead
caught in the gears of a suspected heaven
history becomes a rough draft
its parentheses open and spill

casualties of long ago events
drawn holy into their narrative
a time that was
nestles in the snug coffin
of the time that is

they are coming on the threshold of sleep
to illuminate how to remember
and how to forget

What The Great Almighty Carries In Her Purse

address book of dreams for unkempt minds
keys to the secret laboratory of language
tinted glasses of contentment and despair
sewing kit with safety pins for newly created ruins
tape measure for the metrics of uselessness
cash and change for the noisy whimsy of commerce
mirror to apply the shadows of incomprehension
arbitrary and deliberate facts made of soft rouge
comb to unknot the fundamentals of solitude
photo of family at the well-laid table of reminiscence
tissues for proof of a second icier world

Memoir

on a perfectly drawn line
the garment of self
is hung with graphite and stars

written with air
time scribbles
the fabric of personal history

margins contain
selected collisions
of light and heavy words

between clouds and abyss
a story threadbare and familiar
is scribed with erasable lines

On the Block

in a dim-light meander
a writer's concern for precision,
compression, lyrical sound
and one simple elemental truth
goes down a very bad path

through the double lens
of imagination and memory
a flawed and flimsy
lower case moment
will be mugged

twisted turns of interpretation
coerce a deeper register of inquiry
concluding with a neat ending
and ... oh, could it be ... indelibility

pending yet another bon mot
from an empty poet
the dim light of the computer cursor
blinks on and on
ready to surrender all its belongings
to a merciful delete

A Non Violent Overthrow of Personal History

over a full day and night
years shorten and fly
another decade travels through

no moment ever the same
whirring specks of time
unfurl a wordless backstory

a voice calling itself I
in a sustained oversimplification
grapples with the ineffable

it will always be
too soon
for the open sky
to offer no freedom

reconsidered in light
reconsidered in shadow
it is just life
and then it is over

In Case You Plan to Write a Poem

activate the fluency of perception
excavate memories of ancient wounds
fixate on your own interests
delicately calibrate a lack of artifice

shake off narrative vigorously
curdle pathologies into bon mots
come perilously close to nonsense
snip the stitches of a warm glow

tinker with stubborn question marks
ignore evidence of difficult terrain
extol the virtues of enticement
barrel down pointless roads

and... if that doesn't suffice
reference a moonless night
on a still warm autumn eve

At the Edge

at the edge of awareness
the dead gather
speak in extinct tongues
enter dreams to tell and tell

they seep unrecognized
in the light and in the dark
lacking sufficient ballast
to remain in the knowable

in this one for certain life
the living gather and mourn
they hover and flit
cover the mirrors   rend their clothes

in the surly bonds of earth
it is a love story
with a swamp of confusion
and a lot of ache

while at the edge of awareness
accommodating angels
play with contradictions
and speak in clouds

Acknowledgements

Many thanks to the editors of the publications in which some of these poems first appeared, often in an earlier version. As... I cannot keep from editing them even after publication.

A Room of Her Own: Advice from Mother on Your One Less Day
Bethlehem Writers Group: The Much More
California Poetry Society Quarterly: Borderlands, Dad,
Camroc: In Our Story, Unvarnished
Chatsworth Press: A Baptism in Time
Crannog: At the Edge
EAB: While
Frogmore Papers: I Have Been Thinking
GoldDust Magazine: Heroes
Hartskill Review: Memoir
Inscape: Seriously
Kenyon Review: Recipes
Magnolia Press: Late Night Elegy
Marin Poetry Center: A Fitful Flame, Bitter Feast, Cue the Bagpipes, Dottie, 15 Minutes, Mourning Meditation, Naked Little Creatures, The Daily News, Time in Jeopardy (hey... it's my home county)
Lost Reflections: Dad's 99th Birthday
Nazim Hikmet Festival 6th Annual Contest Winner: Come Summer Stay Summer, Intent of Restoring Disorder, On the Block
Next Review: Whenever
OSU Literary Magazine: A Good Day for Obituaries
Oxford Literary Magazine: Bifocals
Pacific Review: … And Yet
Queen's Head: In Case You Plan to Write a Poem, Beelzebub's Fundamentals for Success
Redwood Writers: At Night, At Sea, Come Sit Stay, Loose Magic, More Holes than Fabric, To Answer Rachel's Question, Today in Yoga, Trick or Treat, When I Die
Reverberations: Billboard for Rent
RiverLit: A Non Violent Overthrow of Personal History
Sin Fronteras. Writers Without Borders: She
Sketchbook Literary Magazine: Milk Bone
Spillway: I Really Should Have Asked

Stoneboat: According to the Arc of the Sun, How to Build a Heart in the Rushed Momentum of Life, Sewing Lesson, The Balloon Escapes the Grasp, This Year, What the Great Almighty Carries in Her Purse, Your Call is Important... Please Hold
The Phoenix: Stay
The Stray Branch: The Chemo Chronicles
Vox Poetica: Everyday
Wax Poetry: The Archangel of Damage
Waywords literary Magazine: What!?
Yes Poetry: Ordinary Light

Les Bernstein's poems have appeared in journals, presses and anthologies in the U.S.A. and internationally. Her chapbooks *Borderland, Naked Little Creatures* and *Amid the Din* have been published Finishing Line Press. Les is a winner of the 6th annual Nazim Hikmet Festival.

She also was a Pushcart Prize Nominee for 2015. Les has been the editor of *Redwood Writer's* anthologies for 2018, 2019, 2020 and 2021 and also the editor of the *Marin High School Anthology* 2018. She lives in Mill Valley with her enormous lovable family.

www.ingramcontent.com/pod-product-compliance
Lightning Source LLC
Chambersburg PA
CBHW021146090426
42740CB00008B/969